International Labour Office

I0104246

PLACEMENT OF JOB-SEEKERS WITH DISABILITIES

Elements of an Effective Service

Barbara Murray
and
Robert Heron

ILO East Asia Multidisciplinary Advisory Team
ILO Regional Office for Asia and the Pacific
Bangkok

First published 1999
Second Edition 2003

ISBN 92-2-115114-X

Printed in Uruguay

Foreword

People with disabilities seek jobs for much the same reasons as non-disabled people. They wish to earn a living, live independently, and make social contacts. As with other job-seekers, finding a job and progressing in it is important for their self-esteem. Like other job-seekers too, they differ enormously in age, place of residence, personality, educational level, skills, abilities, and aspirations.

Unlike non-disabled people, though, people with disabilities are likely to have faced difficulties in getting an education, and in accessing vocational training and further education. These facts alone cause many disabled people problems when it comes to seeking a job. They also face what is for many an unsurmountable obstacle – the negative attitudes of potential employers about their ability to work and to contribute to the performance of the enterprise.

Employment placement services play a central role in promoting employment opportunities, especially for job-seekers who face particular obstacles in finding a job. Since this guide was first published in 1999 for use by policy-makers and managers in the Asian and Pacific Region, the role of placement services in assisting people with disabilities to enter the labour market has been the focus of increasing global attention. Yet, in many countries, the overall functioning of these services needs to be strenghtened so that they can better identify suitable jobs in the open labour market.

Measures to strengthen employment placement service for persons with disabilities must be set in a solid policy framework and if necessary backed by legislation. A clear operational strategy must be designed to guide implementation. In addition, the employment service needs to form linkages with other government ministries and agencies at a policy level, to ensure that obstacles which disabled people may face are minimized, and that the skills which they offer are relevant to labour market opportunities.

The publication intended for policy-makers and managers in mainstream and dedicated employment placement services, operated by governmental and non-governmental organizations. It examines the strategies which an

iii

effective placement service can adopt and the key components which it should include, as well as the alliances which it needs to develop with other agencies to ensure that it can work effectively. It was developed for use in Asia and the Pacific by Barbara Murray, Senior Specialist in Vocational Rehabilitatin, and Robert Heron, former Senior Labour Administration Specialist, ILO EASMAT. Valuable contributions were made, at an early stage, by participants at a technical consultation "Developing an Effective Service for People with Disabilities" held in Singapore, February 1999 and at a workshop "Placing People with Disabilities to Employment" held in Hong Kong, China, March 1999.

It is hoped that this publication, along with the ILO guide for job placement personnel 'Assisting People with Disabilities in Finding Employment' and the ILO Resource Book for trainers of placement officers will contribute to strengthening placement services and to improving opportunities for job seekers with disabilities throughout the Asian and Pacific Region region.

Girma Agune
Director a.i.
Skills Department
ILO
Geneva
October 2003

Table of contents

1

Placement services for people with disabilities – international trends

Employment opportunities for people with disabilities have changed dramatically over the past twenty years. In the past, many disabled job-seekers could only hope to find work alongside other disabled people in special centres, variously known as:

- sheltered workshops

- welfare enterprises

- production workshops.

In recent years, there has been a significant shift to promoting job opportunities for disabled persons in the open labour market, with supports where necessary. There are several reasons for this, but two stand out:

- changed understanding of 'disability'

- the growing cost of excluding disabled people.

Changed understanding of disability

Underlying the trend to open employment is the realization that many of the obstacles which disabled people face arise not from their disability itself, but rather from the way society is organized. Barriers which often prevent disabled people from getting jobs include:

- restrictive rules and regulations relating to training or employment

- work practices which are impossible for people with certain disabilities to observe

- inaccessible workplaces

- the assumptions, often negative, which employers and others make about the abilities and working capacity of disabled people.

These barriers can be overcome, and the employment placement service has an important role to play in this.

Costs of exclusion

Over the past two decades, a clearer understanding has also developed of the economic implications of excluding disabled people from the labour market. The loss of productive capacity by excluding disabled people from the workforce is enormous. In addition, the cost of providing benefits and welfare services for this large and growing group is very high and has become unaffordable in many countries. These countries now recognize that, by opening opportunities for disabled people in the labour force, this cost burden can be significantly reduced, while at the same time disabled workers can live independently and contribute to the national economy.

> The annual value of time lost as a result of chronic disabilities of working-aged Canadians was estimated at 13.9 billion Canadian dollars in 1986. The value of time lost due to short-term disabilities was 2 billion Canadian dollars.

A. Promotional measures

Measures to promote employment opportunities have taken a variety of forms.

- Some countries rely on persuasive support measures in convincing employers to give people with disabilities an opportunity to prove their work capacity.

- Other countries have introduced legislation or regulations to require employers to reserve a certain proportion of jobs for disabled people – generally referred to as quota legislation.

As a result of these efforts, it is increasingly recognized that people with disabilities have a valuable contribution to make to company performance, and more broadly to the national economy, if:

- they have the right skills,

- are placed in the right jobs, and

- are given appropriate supports, if required.

B. Establishment of job placement services

Alongside these developments, employment placement services catering to disabled job-seekers have been established and have expanded. Frequently, these services were started as specialist services catering only to job-seekers with disabilities. This is still considered the most appropriate format in many countries. Examples of specialist employment services in the Asian and Pacific region are:

- China Disabled Persons' Federation Employment Services Centres

- BIZLINK Ltd, Singapore

- the Selective Placement Division of the Hong Kong, China, Labour Department.

Over time, however, given the large number of disabled people seeking jobs and the fact that many of them do not require special service supports, the general employment placement services in many countries have started to cater to disabled people alongside other job-seekers. Some developing countries – such as Viet Nam – have opted for this approach from the start. Some countries – like Thailand and Malaysia – combine an integrated service for all job-seekers with a special placement service for disabled people. In Sweden, the general service for all job-seekers is combined with a special service for those with additional requirements, including job-seekers with disabilities and certain other groups of job-seekers – older workers, immigrant workers, young workers, and other target groups requiring special services. The decision on whether the placement service should be a specialist or a general service rests with the national authorities.

The question of whether jobs can be found for all disabled job-seekers through a specialist service, or whether the general employment service should have a role to play has been debated in many countries, not simply because of the large number of job-seekers with disabilities involved, but also because of the trend towards mainstreaming and inclusion. As a result, it is increasingly accepted that a strategy which combines access to a general service with access to a specialist service, where necessary, is needed if the problem of unemployment among people with disabilities is to be effectively tackled within a reasonable time frame.

C. Ministerial responsibility

Traditionally, responsibility for disability-related policy and programmes has been the responsibility of the ministry of social welfare or the ministry of health, and this is still the case in many countries. With the recent shift in policy along with the changed understanding of disability, responsibility for employment-related policy and services has gradually shifted from these ministries to the ministry of labour. In line with this trend, countries which have just recently established employment services for disabled people have allocated responsibility for these services to the ministry of labour or manpower from the start.

D. The role of NGOs

Non-governmental organizations in many countries have traditionally played an important role in supporting disabled job-seekers in their search for work, often filling a vacuum in the public services in innovative ways. These NGOs continue to provide placement services and should be seen as a valuable resource, supplementing the work of the public placement services.

> **The public employment service can benefit from the placement experience of the NGOs and the networks they have established in finding jobs for disabled people.**

2   Policy and legislative framework for an effective placement service

International instruments and initiatives have played a key role in influencing policy and legislative frameworks at the national level to promote employment opportunities for disabled people. These international initiatives include:

- the World Programme of Action Concerning Disabled Persons, adopted by the United Nations in 1982

- the United Nations Decade of Disabled Persons 1983 - 1992

- the United Nations Standard Rules for the Equalisation of Opportunities for People with Disabilities, adopted in 1993

- the International Labour Organization Convention No. 159 concerning Vocational Rehabilitation and Employment (Disabled Persons) of 1983, its accompanying Recommendation (No.168), 1983 and Recommendation No. 99 concerning Vocational Rehabilitation of the Disabled of 1955

- the Asian and Pacific Decade of Disabled Persons 1993–2002

- the Copenhagen Declaration on Social Development of 1995.

All these initiatives aim to promote the full participation of disabled persons in all aspects and sectors of society, with the Copenhagen Declaration moving a step forward, in viewing disability as a form of social diversity and pointing to the need for an inclusive response which aims to build a 'society for all'.

The ILO Convention views disability as a condition of occupational disadvantage which can and should be overcome through a variety of policy measures, regulations, programmes, and services. It calls upon countries to base their national policies on the principles of:

- equality of opportunity

- equality of treatment

- mainstreaming of training and employment opportunities

- community participation

- tripartite consultations involving public authorities, worker and employer representatives

- consultations with representatives of and for disabled persons.

ILO Recommendations 168 and 99 outline specific measures which might be introduced at the national level to promote employment opportunities for disabled people and call for these to conform to the employment and salary standards applicable to workers generally. The full text of ILO Convention 159 and Recommendations 168 and 99 is reproduced in Annex 1.

A. Policy or legislation?

Some countries make a distinction between policy pronouncements and legislative interventions and others consider policy and legislation to be one and the same. But there is some benefit in distinguishing between them because of their legal implications and related enforcement arrangements.

Policy

A **policy** concerning the employment of disabled persons usually refers to a written document that has three general characteristics.

- It is a broad statement of intention as presented in a parliamentary paper or ministerial document.

- It provides general guidelines for action and implementation, but does not provide the detail required to enable those guidelines to be effectively applied.

- In itself, it is not legally binding, requiring that legislation be introduced to give positive and detailed expression to the policy guidelines and enable the policy to be translated into meaningful action through legal compliance and enforcement.

Example:

The Government will encourage the employment of disabled persons through the introduction of a quota system requiring medium-sized and larger enterprises, both public and private, to allocate a fixed percentage of jobs to disabled persons.

This is a statement of intent that will require some detailed fleshing out if it is to become operational. The law provides this detail through specific legislation which includes:

- a definition of medium-sized and large enterprises

- a definition of disabled persons

- details of the size of the quota (e.g. 5% of all employees; 5% of all employees where the company employs 200 people or more)

- a compliance requirement on time limitations and the penalties for non-compliance

- enforcement procedures, including the relevant agency empowered to enforce the law and punish those enterprises failing to comply.

Some countries with quota schemes

Asia and Pacific	Western Europe	Eastern Europe
China	Austria	the Czech Republic
India	Belgium	Hungary
Japan	Cyprus	Poland
Mongolia	France	Slovakia
Sri Lanka	Germany	
Thailand	Greece	
	Iceland	
	Italy	
	Malta	
	the Netherlands	
	Spain	
	Portugal	
	Turkey	

Example:

The Government will encourage the employment of disabled persons by increasing their opportunities for self-employment in both the formal and non-formal sectors.

This, too, is a statement of intention which, in itself, cannot be enforced because of the lack of operational detail. New laws or regulations will need to be in place if such a pol cy is to be effective.

- What is meant by self-employment?

- What is the definition of a *disabled person*?

- How will the Government provide encouragement? Will it give financial incentives, advisory services, or both?

- What will be the duration of the assistance?

Legislation

Legislation concerning the employment of disabled persons refers to laws, regulations, decrees, notices, and directives that are legally binding and thus give rise to a legal obligation for affected parties to comply.

Some laws include a preamble which sets out the purpose and objectives of the law and which, though inc uded in the law, is more in the nature of a policy statement.

Legislation provides the legal support for policy initiatives, without which policy intentions would not be achieved.

Some examples of specific articles of laws concerning the employment of disabled persons are:

- Article 30 of the Law of the People's Republic of China on the Protection of Disabled Persons (1990) which states that state organs, non-governmental organizations, enterprises, institutions, and urban and rural collective economic organizations shall employ a certain proportion of disabled persons in appropriate types of jobs and posts, with the specific proportion being determined by the governments of provinces and autonomous regions

- Section 11 (1) of the Hong Kong, China, Disability Discrimination Ordinance which states that it is unlawful for a person ('the employer') to discriminate against another person with a disability (a) in the arrangements the employer makes for the purpose of determining who should be offered that employment; (b) in the terms on which the employer offers that other person that employment; or (c) by refusing or deliberately omitting to offer that other person that employment.

- Section 17 (2) of the Rehabilitation of Disabled Persons Act (1991) of Thailand which specifies that employers or owners of private companies shall employ disabled persons suitable to the nature of work at an appropriate ratio to other employees

- Article 21 (1) of the Ordinance on Disabled Persons of the Socialist Republic of Viet Nam which states that administrative and non-business agencies must not refuse job applicants who are disabled persons and who meet all the criteria for suitable jobs for which the agency has the need of recruitment.

- Article 14.5 of the Law for the Employment Promotion of Disabled Persons in Japan, which specifies that certain employers shall, once a year, in accordance with the Ministry of Labour Ordinance, report the employment situation of workers who are physically or intellectually disabled to the Minister of Labour (Law No. 123 of 1960 and Law No. 32 of 1997, revising this Law).

Effective legislation should:

- be clear and unambiguous (which is not always true in the examples shown)

- be sufficiently detailed to clearly identify who is covered by the law and who is excluded

- not provide for too many exceptions or exemptions

- stipulate the agency responsible for enforcement

- indicate the penalties for non-compliance.

Some countries concentrate on policy and education to encourage the employment of persons with disabilities (e.g. Singapore); others concentrate on legislation and enforcement (e.g. Japan), while others try to combine both approaches (e.g. Thailand).

B. Operational strategy

Policy and legislation on employing people with disabilities will have no impact on job opportunities if they are not effectively implemented. An operational strategy is required to ensure that these have a practical impact.

Background information

Planning for the development of an effective and equitable placement service for disabled job-seekers requires certain background information about the dimensions of the service need. The most important questions to be addressed are:

- How many people with disabilities are there of working age?

- How many are capable of work?

- How many are already at work?

- How many are seeking jobs or wish to start a small business?

If this information is not readily available, it may be necessary to proceed based on estimates until a reliable survey can be conducted. Generally, an estimate of between 5 and 7 per cent of the labour force will give an indication of the number of disabled persons of working age, although some downward adjustment may be necessary since some disabled people may be unable to work.

The answers to these questions, together with resource availability, will influence decisions on various operational aspects of the placement service, including:

- strategic emphases

- components

- linkages to other agencies.

Strategic emphases

The operational strategy to implement the goal of promoting open employment opportunities for job-seekers with disabilities sets the framework for the placement service. In particular, it will indicate whether the service will:

- be a dedicated or multi-task service

- be a general or a special service

- take a collective or an individual approach

- involve direct service or self-service.

These strategic emphases will influence the shape of the placement service, and the extent and nature of its linkages with other service providers.

Dedicated or multi-task

In many countries, labour officials are required to undertake a range of tasks in addition to job placement. These include:

- labour inspection and law enforcement

- dispute resolution

- processing and investigation of worker complaints

- processing workers' compensation claims.

This multi-tasking is particularly common at provincial and district levels and reflects the limited staff resources available for labour administration at these levels.

But a dedicated service, in which labour officials are responsible for job placement and related services only, has a number of advantages. These include:

- improved opportunities for developing productive relations with enterprises and for providing them with a quality placement service

- avoiding the contradictory roles of multi-tasked labour officials who will be involved in inspection and law enforcement on one day, and persuasion and negotiation with the employer on another

- an increase in the number of placements due to available time being devoted to one task

- improved opportunity to develop technical expertise relating to placing disabled persons.

General or special

Policy-makers and managers need to decide whether the placement service for job-seekers with disabilities will be part of a general service, open to all job-seekers, or whether it will be a specialist service, open only to people with disabilities.

Traditionally, many countries have provided a placement service for disabled job-seekers using specialists. But attempts are now being made to integrate the service for people with disabilities into the mainstream service open to the general population. This shift in emphasis is due to:

- changes in the understanding of disability

- changes in the policy environment for people with disabilities

- the quantification of the number of disabled job-seekers.

The development of an integrated or general placement service has been combined in many countries with a special service for those disabled persons who need additional support.

Many developing countries have only recently introduced an employment placement service for disabled persons. Often, though, the number of job-seekers with disabilities is so large that a small-scale special service needs to cooperate closely with the general employment service centres. This cooperation is essential if unemployment is to be significantly reduced in the foreseeable future.

> **In China, for example, 7.54 million disabled people (30% of the disabled population of working age) need jobs. In Indonesia, an estimated 2.2 million disabled people are capable of employment.**

In some countries, job-seekers with disabilities first attend the general employment service. If they have special needs which cannot be catered for within this service, they are referred to a more specialist service for people with disabilities only, or to job-seekers with special requirements, whether or not they have a disability (e.g. Sweden).

Collective or individual

Another strategic question is whether the employment service will be provided individually to disabled job-seekers and to employers, or whether it will work through organizations of employers or disabled people, so as to reach a wider audience with the same resources. Once again, the consideration here is one of effectiveness in finding jobs for all unemployed disabled job-seekers.

Under an **individual** approach, for example, job-seekers are prepared for jobs one-to-one, involving regular and direct contact with a placement officer, rather than through group sessions arranged for this purpose.

Under a **collective** approach, the placement service works through employers' organizations or networks to involve more employers in providing jobs and work trials. A collective approach would also include holding seminars and meetings to gain agreement from employer representatives on a partnership approach to improving employment opportunities for disabled persons.

Direct service or self-service

A further important question is whether the placement service officers should provide a direct service to all job-seekers who approach the service, or whether an element of self-service should be involved, with job-seekers gathering information first and then deciding whether they need to contact a placement officer.

If a **direct** approach is taken to service provision, all job-seekers will be:

- interviewed

- registered

- assessed

- matched (if possible)

- referred to an employer

- placed in a job, if the employer considers the applicant to be suitable.

This process will apply to all job-seekers who approach the placement service expressing interest in employment, even if they are capable of finding a job by themselves.

If the placement process is to include an element of **self-service**, job-seekers may:

- respond to job vacancy announcements displayed at the employment service without any assistance from a placement officer

- respond to a job vacancy on the Internet after being notified by the employment service but without any assistance from a placement officer

- select brochures and pamphlets displayed at the employment service to learn more about job preparation courses, special employment assistance programmes, or skill development opportunities

- view a video for guidance on career opportunities.

If additional information or advice is required after the initial self-service, the job-seeker can make an appointment with a placement officer and receive direct and individual assistance.

This approach, which is reflected in the recent trend to establish 'one-stop shops', is likely to reduce the workload of individual job placement officers. As an initiative, however, its effectiveness in terms of outcomes needs to be monitored.

3 Placement service – key components

An effective placement service for people with disabilities should include the following components:

- preparation for jobs

- job placement

- self-employment supports

- publicity

- monitoring and evaluation.

The operational strategy developed at the outset will guide decisions about the form in which each component service is offered, and whether the component service is provided by the placement service itself or by another service provider with which the placement service will closely link (see Chapter 5). Whatever their format, each of these components should be linked to form an effective network of services to promote job placement for disabled job-seekers, rather than operating in isolation.

A. Preparation for jobs

The main elements of a service that prepares a disabled job-seeker for placement are:

- vocational assessment

- skills training

- pre-placement guidance

- promotion of job-seeking skills

- work experience in production units

- on-the-job work trials.

Not all disabled job-seekers will need to avail of all of these services. But each service should be available to ensure that the various needs of people with different types of disabilities are provided for, and that the job-seeker has a greater chance of securing and retaining a job.

Vocational assessment

Where a disabled job-seeker has not previously worked or when a worker is returning to employment following an accident or the onset of a disability, the placement officer may require information on aptitudes, abilities, and working capacity to guide the search for a suitable job. This information may be obtained through a vocational assessment, which usually involves:

- standardized tests to assess intelligence, interests, manual dexterity, mechanical and other aptitudes (such as the ability to distinguish shapes, colours, and sizes).

- practical tests to assess the individual's performance in a variety of jobs such as the ability to concentrate, work speed, and ability to lift weights.

Alternatively, the vocational assessment may be carried out simply by observing someone's performance on a job over a period of time – as, for example, during a placement in a production unit or sheltered workshop. Often, both methods are combined to give a comprehensive picture.

The assessment results are then compared with job descriptions – contained, for example, in a dictionary of occupational classifications or compiled through job or work analysis (see pp. 28–29) – to determine whether the person is suited to the desired job.

Assessment is often carried out in a vocational assessment unit, located within a special centre or workshop. Sometimes, a team of rehabilitation professionals is involved; sometimes the assessment is carried out by a psychologist or occupational therapist; and sometimes the assessment is carried out by a vocational guidance officer or by a placement officer within the employment placement service.

Skills training

Acquiring a skill which is relevant to current labour market openings is of central importance to any job-seeker. It is particularly important to people with disabilities, since they face considerable competition with non-disabled people in their search for jobs, and the additional obstacle of negative employer attitudes to their working capacity. A placement service can effectively seek jobs for people whose skills and qualifications match employer requirements.

Skills training has been traditionally provided for disabled people in special centres. Increasingly, though, there is an emphasis on opening up opportunities for them in the mainstream training centres, or on developing on-the-job training opportunities. These approaches will help to ensure that disabled people have the same opportunities as non-disabled people. It will also help overcome the problems faced in many special centres, which are often constrained by limited resources when it comes to employing instructors, buying training equipment and tools, and ensuring that the centre's courses reflect current and emerging labour market opportunities locally and regionally.

Employment service officers are ideally placed to:

- channel information to training centres about the skills required for employment

- provide them with feedback on the skills of centre graduates, after placement

- arrange on-the-job training for centre graduates, so that they can gradually become accustomed to the pace and procedures of work in the open labour market

- arrange customized training where the employment service has sufficient resources.

Promoting job-seeking skills

If the operational strategy includes an emphasis on enabling job-seekers to find jobs for themselves – on self-service, in addition to direct service – then it is useful to provide training in job-seeking skills for those who need it. This is often done in the form of 'job clubs' where disabled people learn how to write their CV, seek jobs in the newspapers, fill in an application form, develop their telephone skills, and perform well at a job interview. The job clubs may be run by the employment service, or by other service providers contracted to do so. Organizations of people with disabilities may be involved in running these clubs, with the advantage that this provides the opportunity to develop peer support networks.

If possible, job-seekers should have access to the facilities which they need to carry out their own job search – newspapers, a computer, a telephone – and to advice and support where necessary. These facilities could be provided in a 'one-stop shop', where job-seekers can avail themselves of a range of different services related to placement.

Production units

Many people with disabilities benefit from a period of working or training in a special production unit, before they seek jobs in the open labour market. This enables them to get into the habit of working and to develop their working capacity. It can also be useful to placement officers and vocational assessment personnel, enabling them to see how the person performs on different jobs over a longer period, thus complementing the information obtained through vocational assessment.

It is desirable, however, that placement officers do everything possible to ensure that disabled persons are given the opportunity and encouragement to move from a 'sheltered' environment to supported employment or open employment.

Work trials

Work trials in companies are another way of testing the capacity of disabled job-seekers to hold down jobs in the open labour market, and of introducing them gradually to employers who may be reluctant to offer a more permanent job. The placement service may arrange work trials for people who approach the service directly, or for trainees attending skills training centres. The work trial is useful in demonstrating the disabled person's ability and working capacity to employers, who may offer them a job after the trial period. In other cases, it provides the opportunity for the person to obtain a reference which they can add to their CV, to assist them in their subsequent job search. Where the disabled person does not successfully complete the work trial, the placement service may advise further training or guidance.

B. Job placement

These steps are involved in job placement:

- gathering information on job vacancies, and on job-seekers

- making contacts with employers

- providing technical advice

- conducting job and work analysis

- job-matching

- job-coaching

- providing follow-up services.

Gathering information

- **on job vacancies**

The placement service requires a system for gathering information on local job vacancies as they emerge. This may involve notification from employers, combined with use of newspaper job advertisements, and information gained through personal contacts with employers. This information should include the job title, along with a description of tasks and working conditions, including working time, pay, and holidays. Placement services have in the past recorded this information manually, but the trend is now to computerize it where possible, for ease and speed of retrieval. This enables job placement officers to identify suitable jobs for job-seekers with minimal delay. It may also form the basis of an information service for disabled job-seekers who can conduct their own job search.

If a computerized approach is to be introduced, its resource implications – financial and human – need to be considered and planned for.

For some disabled job-seekers, additional information may be required about the jobs in question, such as company location, accessibility of the company premises, availability of public transport, and company policy towards employing disabled people. This information should be gathered when discussing the placement with the employer.

Information on job vacancies should be complemented by information on local labour market trends. This may be gathered by the placement service directly or through other agencies who monitor these trends, and by visiting local enterprises. The key information concerns:

- which enterprises are growing

- which are contracting

- what technological changes are taking place and

- how these will affect jobs.

- **on job-seekers**

Information should be obtained on individual job-seekers'

- educational level

- qualifications

- skills and experience

- disabilities and work-related needs associated with this

- occupational aspirations.

This information should be obtained primarily from the job-seekers or their advocates. Some information may be required from vocational assessment professionals to indicate work capacity and aptitudes; sometimes medical reports may provide additional information about the person's disability as it affects capacity to work. But this information should be sought after the first interview with the job-seeker, whose agreement to access the information should first be obtained.

The information on job-seekers should be recorded either on card or on computer. This is called the process of registration, which should be kept as simple as possible. Job-seekers should be encouraged to re-register at regular intervals by phone or by letter if they have not found a suitable job. They should also be encouraged to inform the placement service if they find a job through other means.

Contacting employers

Employers are important clients of the placement service which should invest resources in developing a partnership with them. In cooperation with employers, placement officers can place job-seekers to existing job vacancies and assist in creating new opportunities for disabled job-seekers.

Depending on the placement service strategy, employers may be contacted individually and through associations of employers, industry associations (e.g. hotel and tourism, manufacturers, financial services), and chambers of commerce. Informal networks of employers may also be tapped to contact other employers who may be willing to provide an opportunity of some sort to disabled people – a work trial, on-the-job training, a supported-employment placement, or a job.

Contacting individual employers

Employers should be regarded as valued clients of the job placement service, and as potential partners. They require high-quality service from the placement service to help them identify suitable employees for their vacant positions. In return for this service, they may provide valuable advice on skills training, in identifying jobs, and in establishing viable small businesses.

Placement officers need to be able to **"think like an employer"** so as to negotiate effectively with them. The placement service should foster this awareness through training. It should also develop an employer database, containing as much information as possible about companies in its catchment area, including their policies and practices concerning employing disabled people. Informational brochures and technical materials should be developed, providing the employer with relevant information about the work ability of disabled persons as well as the placement service itself, in an attractive, easy-to-read format.

Contacting employers' associations

Working through employer associations may prove extremely effective. At a policy level, it is useful to develop an agreement with these associations to cooperate in promoting employment opportunities for disabled people. Such an agreement would require the involvement of policy-makers within the employment service as a whole. At a practical level, cooperation could take the form of seminars or meetings, jointly organized with the employer association, drawing on the association's membership for ideas about how the topic should be approached. Such events, if well planned, are likely to have far greater impact in opening doors to individual employers than if the placement service were to organize a seminar on its own. Alternatively, it could take the form of an agreement reached with the employer association to provide job placements and work trials through its member companies. Working in this way, the placement service can contact far more employers, more efficiently, than if each were to be contacted individually.

Using employer networks

In addition to working with formal employer networks, the placement service may develop informal networks. For example, it could ask employers who have successfully employed people with disabilities to act as advocates in persuading other employers to give a disabled person a work-related opportunity. The placement service could then follow up on the contacts. Employer advocates could also provide valuable advice on the skills and work-related behaviour required of employees, which the placement service can pass on to the skills training providers.

> **Employers are more likely to listen to other employers than to placement officers.**

Work and job analysis

The ability to identify suitable jobs for job-seekers with disabilities is central to an effective placement service. This requires job placement officers to be able to carry out:

- work analysis and

- job analysis.

Work analysis involves looking at all work carried out in an enterprise or in one department or section.

The purpose is to:

- identify elements of **existing** jobs which could be combined into one or more new jobs suitable for a disabled person

- identify work which is not being done at all, which could become the basis for a new job to be performed by a disabled person

- identify **opportunities** for work experience programmes for disabled persons.

Job analysis involves looking at existing jobs to find out what the worker does, how the work is done, where it is done, what skills and abilities are required, and the conditions under which it is done. To carry out job analysis, it is necessary to:

- observe the work carried out in the enterprise as a whole

- observe the work being done in a particular job

- interview workers, supervisors, and personnel managers and

- listen to workers, other disabled persons, supervisors, and managers.

The purpose is to assess:

- which jobs could be done by disabled persons should future vacancies occur

- which jobs could be done by disabled persons if the job or the working environment was modified in some way

- which parts of a job could be done by a disabled person if a job restructuring was to take place.

> **It is important that job placement officers receive training and practical experience, so that they can carry out job and work analysis effectively.**

Technical advice

Employers who are willing to consider engaging a disabled person or providing a work trial require information and advice which the placement service should be ready to provide. This includes:

- information on laws, quotas, financial assistance, and other support measures concerning the employment of disabled persons

- information on various disabilities and their implications, if any, for the individual's working capacity

- information and advice on safety and accessibility for workers with different types of disability

- advice on adaptations to workplaces, workstations, and work procedures

- advice on the effect on co-workers and supervisors of employing people with disabilities of different kinds.

Being able to provide this advice and information when requested is central to the effectiveness of the placement service and will greatly enhance its credibility with employers. If the information is not already available, a technical desk-manual should be developed for use by job placement officers, and informational brochures should be developed specifically for employers, communicating the necessary information clearly, simply, and in an attractive format.

Job matching

The ability to match job-seekers with suitable jobs is central to the work of the placement service. Placement officers will draw on information they have gathered about the disabled job-seeker (through interviewing and vocational assessment) and about the job requirements in trying to achieve the best match possible.

Where a perfect match is not immediately possible – if, for example, the disabled job-seeker lacks the necessary experience and training – the employer may be persuaded to offer a work trial to enable the disabled person to acquire the experience and skills needed for the job. Sometimes the employer may offer the person a job on completion of the work trial. In other cases, the work trial can be used in the person's CV and may assist in getting another job ater on, particularly if the first employer provides a reference; or it can be used to identify further training or job preparation which the person may require before securing a job.

Job coaching

Where an employer agrees that a disabled person can be trained on the job – whether as part of a supported employment placement, a work trial, or purely as a training placement – the placement service may be required to arrange for a job coach to provide the training if the employer does not have a supervisor who can do this. The job coach service may be arranged and paid for by the placement service directly, or, more usually, by contracting another agency (often a non-governmental organization) to provide this service. The job coach service may be arranged for whatever time is required. In some cases, several days is sufficient. In others, the coach may need to train the disabled person for a longer period, and possibly provide back-up support, visiting the company regularly after the initial training.

The job-coach service makes on-the-job training possible where the company supervisors are not available. On-the-job coaching has several advantages over conventional training provided before placement in a training centre for people with disabilities:

- The machinery used for training is up-to-date.

- The work processes are those currently in use in the labour market.

- The working conditions are those of a viable company.

Follow-up

Sometimes a follow-up service is essential to ensure that the disabled worker is successful in the job.

Follow-up can assist the disabled worker in keeping the job by identifying any existing or emerging problems and can assist the employer by focusing attention on the disabled worker and the job, with a view to minimizing tensions which may have emerged. The follow-up visit also gives the placement officer the opportunity to explore whether the employer is interested in employing other disabled workers. If the employer is reluctant, this provides a good opportunity to find out why. If the employer is interested, details of possible jobs can be obtained.

Follow-up can require quite a lot of time, so a decision will be needed on which placements to review. Priority should be given to disabled persons in their first job, disabled persons receiving on-the-job training, and disabled persons requiring ongoing support.

C. Self-employment

Supports to self-employment make up a further important element of an effective placement service for people with disabilities. This is particularly true in developing countries where a high percentage of the workforce is engaged in this form of work, either in the formal or informal sector. Self-employment has not received as much attention as other employment options for people with disabilities up to now, although many of those who complete training at special centres go on to try earning a living in this way. Its potential has increased with the development of information technology and the emergence of telework and e-commerce as viable options particularly relevant to people with limited mobility.

Frequently, the only assistance provided to those who wish to set up their own businesses is training in the specific skill involved, along with financial assistance in the form of start-up grants or loans, or in some cases, a grant of machinery or equipment. Often the placement service administers the grants or loans, while training centres issue the tools and equipment.

But for a business to be viable, more is needed than a particular skill or some start-up incentives. Budding entrepreneurs need to know how to identify a business opportunity and develop a business plan. They also need management and bookkeeping skills. They sometimes need access to technical advisory services, and assistance in marketing their products and services. They usually need assistance in accessing credit, and in purchasing raw materials in sufficient bulk to minimize costs. Employment services may provide some of the required support directly, but it is more likely that they will refer the disabled person to other agencies that provide the requisite service, or they may contract other agencies to provide the service for specific individuals.

In advising disabled people about self-employment, it is important that the placement services be discerning, since not everyone has what it takes to become an entrepreneur.

D. Publicity and promotion

Publicity is of central importance to an effective employment service, particularly if it has been decided to take a collective approach to promoting employment opportunities for disabled job-seekers.

The publicity department can work through:

- media events

- seminars

- job bazaars

- publications

- videos.

Strategic alliances may be formed with other partners to assist the placement service in its promotional work. Media groups and advertising agencies could be approached to assist in the development of a Code of Practice for the portrayal of people with disabilities, and to advise on designing effective awareness-raising campaigns targeted at specific groups – primarily employers. The support of journalists and marketers could be enlisted in designing and writing promotional brochures intended for employers. By cooperating with professionals in these fields, the placement service will become more effective in conveying a positive image of disabled workers and overcoming negative attitudes.

4

Monitoring and evaluation

A comprehensive employment service for people with disabilities involves many different levels and component parts, as illustrated in Diagram 1 (p. 41). Effective management of this service requires a monitoring and evaluation system to help ensure that:

- the service is delivered in line with objectives

- **planned** service outcomes become **actual** outcomes.

Monitoring involves the systematic collection of information about the service to check its operation and observe its progress over time.

Evaluation involves making judgements about the service, based on comprehensive information on current performance. Comparisons may be made with past performance or with targets set.

A. Why is monitoring and evaluation important?

Monitoring and evaluation are increasingly part of management practice in publicly funded activities. They are useful in:

- assessing effectiveness (Is the service working?)

- identifying strengths and weaknesses (What needs to be improved, what needs to be changed?)

- assessing efficiency (Is it 'value for money'?).

Information obtained in this way is a valuable tool for managers and policy-makers in the placement service, enabling them to have a regular overview of service performance, to identify any problem areas which need attention, and to take timely corrective action.

Monitoring and evaluation are particularly important in managing a service which includes so many different component parts, since the performance of one section may have an impact on the performance of others. The information generated can make this link apparent, identify the source of the problem, and provide the basis for a solution.

B. How is monitoring and evaluation carried out?

The goals and objectives of the employment service provide the framework for the monitoring and evaluation system. In developing this system, several steps are involved:

- The stated objectives of the service are translated into measurable terms.

- Indicators of performance which fully reflect service delivery and outcomes are identified and agreed with relevant stakeholders.

- Information is gathered systematically, often over a period of time, from service providers and users.

- The information is analyzed.

- Comparisons are made.

- Judgements are formed.

- The findings are presented.

- Recommendations for change are made, if necessary.

Measureable objectives

Some employment service objectives are stated in terms which are easy to measure. Examples are objectives

- to place disabled job-seekers to employment

- to assist employers in filling vacancies.

Other objectives are less amenable to measurement – for example, where a service objective is:

- to promote awareness among employers of the working ability and capacity of disabled people

- to help job-seekers to find jobs which best suit their abilities, by providing vocational guidance and assessment

- to enable job-seekers to find jobs by providing training in job-seeking skills and access to related facilities.

Such broad, intangible objectives need to be translated into terms which will allow their achievement to be measured, either through statistics (quantitatively) or description (qualitatively), before the monitoring and evaluation can start.

Performance indicators

Identifying indicators which will mirror how well the employment service meets its objectives is a crucial step in developing the monitoring and evaluation system.

Where the objectives are easy to measure quantitatively, it may be relatively easy to identify and agree the relevant indicators. Examples are:

- the number of job-seekers with different disabilities registered with the service

- the number of employers contacted

- the number of job vacancies notified

- the number of placements obtained

- cost per placement.

In developing these indicators, care should be taken to ensure that they reflect the work involved. For example, if a person has a severe disability, more time and effort may be required to secure a placement than in other cases. If statistics are based on a simple 'head count', this extra work will not be reflected. But if the statistics are weighted to reflect the severity of disability or the amount of service time required, a more accurate picture of service performance will be obtained.

Where the objectives are less tangible, a more creative approach is required to develop performance indicators. In addition to statistics, it may be decided to:

- create an indicator of client satisfaction by carrying out regular surveys

- make a video, illustrating aspects of the service

- prepare a photographic exhibition.

Once the performance indicators have been identified, it is important that all relevant decision-makers and managers in the employment service agree that they provide a comprehensive picture of the work carried out and services provided.

Gathering information

The method of gathering the information required for monitoring and evaluation should:

- be as simple as possible

- take as little time as possible

- not interfere with service delivery.

Training should be provided for placement officers to ensure that there is clarity on the information required and the approach to be used.

Making judgements

The monitoring and evaluation information should be regularly compiled and analyzed to form the basis of judgements about service performance over time or in comparison with targets which have been set. It is important to do this regularly so that the findings and judgements do not come as a surprise.

Communicating the findings

Generally, evaluation results are presented as a report. If this is lengthy, it is useful to prepare a shorter summary for wider circulation.

In addition to the written report, evaluation findings may be presented through:

- seminars and workshops targeted at policy-makers

- a photographic exhibition

- video.

C. Who is involved?

An external assessor may be appointed to conduct an evaluation. This may be the case when a funder wishes to verify that the service is being provided according to the agreed format.

Alternatively, an outsider may be called in if the managers or staff do not have the requisite skills.

But increasingly, the tasks of monitoring and evaluating are part of the ongoing work of staff and managers of the service or activity. This approach is often preferred, as it ensures that the service providers are actively involved, and are not apprehensive about the evaluation.

D. How are the outcomes used?

Outcomes of the monitoring and evaluation are useful in:

- establishing whether the service is having the desired impact

- informing decisions to expand or cut back

- identifying ways the service can be improved

- justifying funding requests

- informing policy-makers of any changes which may be required in policy, to promote service effectiveness

- identifying the need for changes in existing law or for the introduction of new laws.

While the outcomes may be used to justify the continuation of the service, their main value lies in helping to **improve** service delivery and outcomes.

Diagram 1

Developing an Effective Placement Service for People with Disabilities

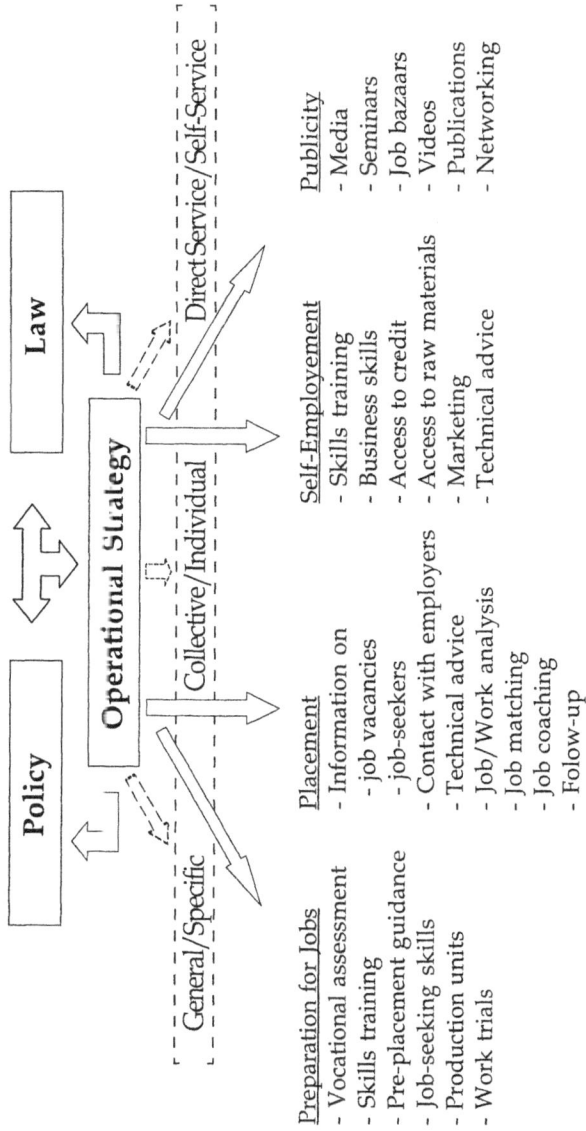

Monitoring & Evaluation

Policy

Law

Operational Strategy

General/Specific

Collective/Individual

Direct Service/Self-Service

Preparation for Jobs
- Vocational assessment
- Skills training
- Pre-placement guidance
- Job-seeking skills
- Production units
- Work trials

Placement
- Information on
  - job vacancies
  - job-seekers
- Contact with employers
- Technical advice
- Job/Work analysis
- Job matching
- Job coaching
- Folow-up

Self-Employement
- Skills training
- Business skills
- Access to credit
- Access to raw materials
- Marketing
- Technical advice

Publicity
- Media
- Seminars
- Job bazaars
- Videos
- Publications
- Networking

5

Building external alliances

The employment service is part of a network of services, associations, and agencies which all have a direct or indirect contribution to make in promoting employment opportunities for people with disabilities (see Diagram 2, p. 48). Linkages within this network, if strategically planned, can assist the service to maximize its effectiveness.

A. Client associations

Linkages with employer organizations can assist the employment service in opening the door to employment for many more disabled job-seekers than would be possible if individual employers were contacted separately. It is increasingly apparent that resources need to be devoted to developing such linkages, given the large number of disabled job-seekers in many countries and the limited resources available to the placement service.

Linkages with organizations of disabled people feature less commonly than those with employer organizations, but in some countries they are now seen as important in providing peer support to job seekers, either informally, or formally through job-seeking skills training (job clubs).

B. Service providers

New approaches to service delivery are being developed in employment services in many countries, because:

- public employment services increasingly lack the resources (staff, funds, facilities) needed to carry out all the activities within their mandate;

- some of the components may be within the mandate of the placement services, but may be more effectively provided by other agencies;

- some of the components may lie outside the mandate of the placement service (such as skills training, promotional activities).

By linking with other agencies, not only will the necessary services be delivered to employers and job-seekers, but the cooperative effort may lead to a greater improvement in employment opportunities than if each of the agencies operated in isolation.

Job placement

The job placement function is carried out by the employment service in all countries, sometimes in collaboration with non-governmental organizations and vocational training centre staff. There is often a benefit from such collaboration, as NGOs frequently have greater flexibility in approach which the public employment service can learn from and build upon. Where the placement service for job-seekers with disabilities is a specialist service which caters only to this target group, then linkages to the mainstream placement service should also be developed.

Other services

Some component services may be provided by the employment service or be the responsibility of skills training centres, NGOs, the social work department of the ministry of health or social welfare, or counselling services provided publicly or privately. Where an external organizaton or agency is involved, the employment service may contact them about providing the service required, or commission them to provide a specific service on behalf of an employment service client. These include:

- skills training

- vocational assessment

- training in job-seeking skills

- self-employment training and supports

- operation of production units

- work trials

- job coaching

- follow-up support

- counselling

- social investigation.

Where the employment service relies on services provided externally, resources should be devoted to:

- negotiating the service for individual clients

- ensuring that the service provided meets the identified need

- providing feedback on the service, drawing on job-seeker and employer comments.

Example:

Through their contacts with employers and their knowledge of labour market trends, placement officers are in a good position to:

- identify skills currently required in the labour market and those likely to be required in the future, in which training is not currently being provided

- give valuable feedback on the relevance of existing training courses and on any changes which might be required.

This information should be passed to the skills training centres, so that graduates from their courses are equipped with up-to-date, employable skills. Placement officers may also be able to assist the training centres in arranging on-the-job training opportunities and work trials in local companies.

The employment service may need to draw on the services of professional counselors and social workers, where the individual job-seekers' requirements or problems go beyond vocational assessment and guidance as generally understood. Placement officers need to learn to recognize when the demands being placed on them by job-seekers go beyond the services they are competent to provide, and when they should call in a professional counselor or social worker.

Sometimes contacts with families of disabled job-seekers are important since the families make up the job-seekers' primary support network and can be invaluable in ensuring that the person gets to work on time, and in providing support if any problems arise. Job placement officers can draw on families in this context, although once again, if the contact with families is for other reasons – such as overprotectiveness of the disabled person – it may be more appropriate for social workers to become involved.

Linkages with other ministries

At a policy level, the employment service can benefit from links with other government ministries – in particular ministries responsible for education, transport, and the built environment. Through these channels, issues relating to literacy, transport, and accessibility which arise in trying to place disabled people to jobs can be brought to the attention of the ministries responsible, which can take steps to improve service.

C. Promotional and developmental work

Media

The employment service may benefit from linkages with the media, and with advertising companies to assist it in its promotional work. Such linkages could be developed for example, as a follow-up to a conference on the image of disabled people in the media, where interested professionals could be invited to form a working group on promoting positive images of workers with disabilities. This could lead not only to a more positive image of disabled people as portrayed in the media, but also to the development of effective promotional materials targeted at potential employers.

Universities, research institutes

Linkages with university departments and research institutes should also be fostered. These may already be conducting research and development projects relating to disability or could be encouraged to do so. Examples are projects to develop technical aids, computer programmes, or devices which can enhance the employment prospects of people with certain types of disability. The assistance of university departments in developing new devices and in other projects to assist disabled people in employment could also be encouraged by involving undergraduate and graduate students in small-scale research and development work in this area.

Diagram 2

Building Strategic Alliances - External

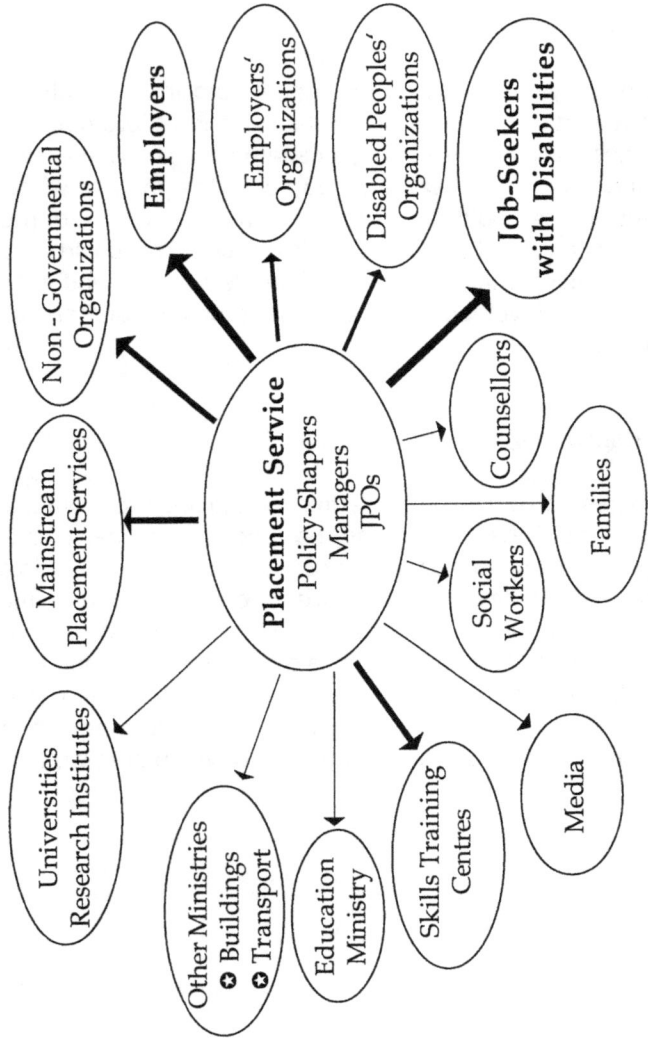

- Employers
- Employers' Organizations
- Disabled Peoples' Organizations
- Job-Seekers with Disabilities
- Non-Governmental Organizations
- Mainstream Placement Services
- Placement Service (Policy-Shapers, Managers, JPOs)
- Counsellors
- Social Workers
- Families
- Universities Research Institutes
- Other Ministries
  - Buildings
  - Transport
- Education Ministry
- Skills Training Centres
- Media

Convention No. 159

CONVENTION CONCERNING VOCATIONAL REHABILITATION AND EMPLOYMENT (DISABLED PERSONS)

The General Conference of the International Labour Organisation,

Having been convened at Geneva by the Governing Body of the International Labour Office and having met in its Sixty-ninth Session on 1 June 1983, and

Noting the existing international standards contained in the Vocational Rehabilitation (Disabled) Recommendation, 1955, and the Human Resources Development Recommendation, 1975, and

Noting that since the adoption of the Vocational Rehabilitation (Disabled) Recommendation, 1955, significant developments have occurred in the understanding of rehabilitation needs, the scope and organisation of rehabilitation services, and the law and practice of many Members on the questions covered by that Recommendation, and

Considering that the year 1981 was declared by the United Nations General Assembly the International Year of Disabled Persons, with the theme "full participation and equality" and that a comprehensive World Programme of Action concerning Disabled Persons is to provide effective measures at the international and national levels for the realisation of the goals of "full participation" of disabled persons in social life and development, and of "equality," and

Considering that these developments have made it appropriate to adopt new international standards on the subject which take account, in particular, of the need to ensure equality of opportunity and treatment to all categories of disabled persons, in both rural and urban areas, for employment and integration into the community, and

Having decided upon the adoption of certain proposals with regard to vocational rehabilitation which is the fourth item on the agenda of the session, and

Having determined that these proposals shall take the form of an international Convention,

adopts this twentieth day of June of the year one thousand nine hundred and eighty-three, the following Convention, which may be cited as the Vocational Rehabilitation and Employment (Disabled Persons) Convention, 1983:

PART I. DEFINITION AND SCOPE

Article 1

1. For the purposes of this Convention, the term "disabled person" means an individual whose prospects of securing, retaining and advancing in suitable employment are substantially reduced as a result of a duly recognised physical or mental impairment.

2. For the purposes of this Convention, each Member shall consider the purpose of vocational rehabilitation as being to enable a disabled person to secure, retain and advance in suitable employment and thereby to further such person's integration or reintegration into society.

3. The provisions of this Convention shall be applied by each Member through measures which are appropriate to national conditions and consistent with national practice.

4. The provisions of this Convention shall apply to all categories of disabled persons.

PART II. PRINCIPLES OF VOCATIONAL REHABILITATION AND
EMPLOYMENT POLICIES FOR DISABLED PERSONS

Article 2

Each Member shall, in accordance with national conditions, practice and possibilities, formulate, implement and periodically review a national policy on vocational rehabilitation and employment of disabled persons.

Article 3

The said policy shall aim at ensuring that appropriate vocational rehabilitation measures are made available to all categories of disabled persons, and at promoting employment opportunities for disabled persons in the open labour market.

Article 4

The said policy shall be based on the principle of equal opportunity between disabled workers and workers generally. Equality of opportunity and treatment for disabled men and women workers shall be respected. Special positive measures aimed at effective equality of opportunity and treatment between disabled workers and other workers shall not be regarded as discriminating against other workers.

Article 5

The representative organisations of employers and workers shall be consulted on the implementation of the said policy, including the measures to be taken to promote co-operation and co-ordination between the public and private bodies engaged in vocational rehabilitation activities. The representative organisations of and for disabled persons shall also be consulted.

PART III. ACTION AT THE NATIONAL LEVEL FOR THE
DEVELOPMENT OF VOCATIONAL REHABILITATION AND
EMPLOYMENT SERVICES FOR DISABLED PERSONS

Article 6

Each Member shall, by laws or regulations or by any other method consistent with national conditions and practice, take such steps as may be necessary to give effect to Articles 2, 3, 4 and 5 of this Convention.

Article 7

The competent authorities shall take measures with a view to providing and evaluating vocational guidance, vocational training, placement, employment and other related services to enable disabled persons to secure, retain and advance in employment; existing services for workers generally shall, wherever possible and appropriate, be used with necessary adaptations.

Article 8

Measures shall be taken to promote the establishment and development of vocational rehabilitation and employment services for disabled persons in rural areas and remote communities.

Article 9

Each Member shall aim at ensuring the training and availability of rehabilitation counsellors and other suitably qualified staff responsible for the vocational guidance, vocational training, placement and employment of disabled persons.

PART IV FINAL PROVISIONS

Article 10

The formal ratifications of this Convention shall be communicated to the Director-General of the International Labour Office for registration.

Article 11

1.   This Convention shall be binding only upon those Members of the International Labour Organisation whose ratifications have been registered with the Director-General.

2.   It shall come into force twelve months after the date on which the ratifications of two Members have been registered with the Director-General.

3.   Thereafter, this Convention shall come into force for any Member twelve months after the date on which its ratification has been registered.

Article 12

1.   A Member which has ratified this Convention may denounce it after the expiration of ten years from the date on which the Convention first comes into force, by an act communicated to the Director-General of the International Labour Office for registration. Such denunciation shall not take effect until one year after the date on which it is registered.

2.   Each Member which has ratified this Convention and which does not, within the year following the expiration of the period of ten years mentioned in the preceding paragraph, exercise the right of denunciation provided for in this Article, will be bound for another period of ten years and, thereafter, may denounce this Convention at the expiration of each period of ten years under the terms provided for in this Article.

Article 13

1. The Director-General of the International Labour Office shall notify all Members of the International Labour Organisation of the registration of all ratifications and denunciations communicated to him by the Members of the Organisation.

2. When notifying the Members of the Organisation of the registration of the second ratification communicated to him, the Director-General shall draw the attention of the Members of the Organisation to the date upon which the Convention will come into force.

Article 14

The Director-General of the International Labour Office shall communicate to the Secretary-General of the United Nations for registration in accordance with Article 102 of the Charter of the United Nations full particulars of all ratifications and acts of denunciation registered by him in accordance with the provisions of the preceding Articles.

Article 15

At such times as it may consider necessary the Governing Body of the International Labour Office shall present to the General Conference a report on the working of this Convention and shall examine the desirability of placing on the agenda of the Conference the question of its revision in whole or in part.

Article 16

1. Should the Conference adopt a new Convention revising this Convention in whole or in part, then, unless the new Convention otherwise provides-

(a) the ratification by a Member of the new revising Convention shall *ipso jure* involve the immediate denunciation of this Convention, notwithstanding the provisions of Article 12 above, if and when the new revising Convention shall have come into force;

(b) as from the date when the new revising Convention comes into force this Convention shall cease to be open to ratification by the Members.

2. This Convention shall in any case remain in force in its actual form and content for those Members which have ratified it but have not ratified the revising Convention.

Article 17

The English and French versions of the text of this Convention are equally authoritative

Recommendation No. 168

RECOMMENDATION CONCERNING VOCATIONAL REHABILITATION AND EMPLOYMENT (DISABLED PERSONS)

The General Conference of the International Labour Organisation,

Having been convened at Geneva by the Governing Body of the International Labour Office and having met in its Sixty-ninth Session on 1 June 1983, and

Noting the existing international standards contained in the Vocational Rehabilitation (Disabled) Recommendation, 1955, and

Noting that since the adoption of the Vocational Rehabilitation (Disabled) Recommendation, 1955, significant developments have occurred in the understanding of rehabilitation needs, the scope and organisation of rehabilitation services, and the law and practice of many Members on the questions covered by that Recommendation, and

Considering that the year 1981 was declared by the United Nations General Assembly the International Year of Disabled Persons, with the theme "full participation and equality" and that a comprehensive World Programme of Action concerning Disabled Persons is to provide effective measures at the international and national levels for the realisation of the goals of "full participation" of disabled persons in social life and development, and of "equality," and

Considering that these developments have made it appropriate to adopt new international standards on the subject which take account, in particular, of the need to ensure equality of opportunity and treatment to all categories of disabled persons, in both rural and urban areas, for employment and integration into the community, and

Having decided upon the adoption of certain proposals with regard to vocational rehabilitation which is the fourth item on the agenda of the session, and

Having determined that these proposals shall take the form of a Recommendation supplementing the Vocational Rehabilitation and Employment (Disabled Persons) Convention, 1983, and the Vocational Rehabilitation (Disabled) Recommendation, 1955,

adopts this twentieth day of June of the year one thousand nine hundred and eighty-three, the following Recommendation, which may be cited as the Vocational Rehabilitation and Employment (Disabled Persons) Recommendation, 1983.

I. DEFINITIONS AND SCOPE

1. In applying this Recommendation, as well as the Vocational Rehabilitation (Disabled) Recommendation, 1955, Members should consider the term "disabled person" as meaning an individual whose prospects of securing, retaining and advancing in suitable employment are substantially reduced as a result of a duly recognised physical or mental impairment.

2. In applying this Recommendation, as well as the Vocational Rehabilitation (Disabled) Recommendation, 1955, Members should consider the purpose of vocational rehabilitation, as defined in the latter Recommendation, as being to enable a disabled person to secure, retain and advance in suitable employment and thereby to further such person's integration or reintegration into society.

3. The provisions of this Recommendation should be applied by Members through measures which are appropriate to national conditions and consistent with national practice.

4. Vocational rehabilitation measures should be made available to all categories of disabled persons.

5. In planning and providing services for the vocational rehabilitation and employment of disabled persons, existing vocational guidance, vocational training, placement, employment and related services for workers generally should, wherever possible, be used with any necessary adaptations.

6. Vocational rehabilitation should be started as early as possible. For this purpose, health-care systems and other bodies responsible for medical and social rehabilitation should co-operate regularly with those responsible for vocational rehabilitation.

II. VOCATIONAL REHABILITATION AND EMPLOYMENT OPPORTUNITIES

7. Disabled persons should enjoy equality of opportunity and treatment in respect of access to, retention of and advancement in employment which, wherever possible, corresponds to their own choice and takes account of their individual suitability for such employment.

8. In providing vocational rehabilitation and employment assistance to disabled persons, the principle of equality of opportunity and treatment for men and women workers should be respected.

9. Special positive measures aimed at effective equality of opportunity and treatment between disabled workers and other workers should not be regarded as discriminating against other workers.

10. Measures should be taken to promote employment opportunities for disabled persons which conform to the employment and salary standards applicable to workers generally.

11. Such measures, in addition to those enumerated in Part VII of the Vocational Rehabilitation (Disabled) Recommendation, 1955, should include:

(a) appropriate measures to create job opportunities on the open labour market, including financial incentives to employers to encourage them to provide training and subsequent employment for disabled persons, as well as to make reasonable adaptations to workplaces, job design, tools, machinery and work organisation to facilitate such training and employment;

(b) appropriate government support for the establishment of various types of sheltered employment for disabled persons for whom access to open employment is not practicable;

(c) encouragement of co-operation between sheltered and production workshops on organisation and management questions so as to improve the employment situation of their disabled workers and, wherever possible, to help prepare them for employment under normal conditions;

(d) appropriate government support to vocational training, vocational guidance, sheltered employment and placement services for disabled persons run by non-governmental organisations;

(e) encouragement of the establishment and development of co-operatives by and for disabled persons and, if appropriate, open to workers generally;

(f) appropriate government support for the establishment and development of small-scale industry, co-operative and other types of production workshops by and for disabled persons (and, if appropriate, open to workers generally), provided such workshops meet defined minimum standards;

(g) elimination, by stages if necessary, of physical, communication and architectural barriers and obstacles affecting transport and access to and free movement in premises for the training and employment of disabled persons; appropriate standards should be taken into account for new public buildings and facilities;

(h) wherever possible and appropriate, facilitation of adequate means of transport to and from the places of rehabilitation and work according to the needs of disabled persons;

(i) encouragement of the dissemination of information on examples of actual and successful instances of the integration of disabled persons in employment;

(j) exemption from the levy of internal taxes or other internal charges of any kind, imposed at the time of importation or subsequently on specified articles, training materials and equipment required for rehabilitation centres, workshops, employers and disabled persons, and on specified aids and devices required to assist disabled persons in securing and retaining employment;

(k) provision of part-time employment and other job arrangements, in accordance with the capabilities of the individual disabled person for whom full-time employment is not immediately, and may not ever be, practicable;

(l) research and the possible application of its results to various types of disability in order to further the participation of disabled persons in ordinary working life;

(m) appropriate government support to eliminate the potential for exploitation within the framework of vocational training and sheltered employment and to facilitate transition to the open labour market.

12. In devising programmes for the integration or reintegration of disabled persons into working life and society, all forms of training should be taken into consideration; these should include, where necessary and appropriate, vocational preparation and training, modular training, training in activities of daily living, in literacy and in other areas relevant to vocational rehabilitation.

13. To ensure the integration or reintegration of disabled persons into ordinary working life, and thereby into society, the need for special support measures should also be taken into consideration, including the provision of aids, devices and ongoing personal services to enable disabled persons to secure, retain and advance in suitable employment.

14. Vocational rehabilitation measures for disabled persons should be followed up in order to assess the results of these measures.

III. Community Participation

15. Vocational rehabilitation services in both urban and rural areas and in remote communities should be organised and operated with the fullest possible community participation, in particular with that of the representatives of employers', workers' and disabled persons' organisations.

16. Community participation in the organisation of vocational rehabilitation services for disabled persons should be facilitated by carefully planned public information measures with the aims of:

(a) informing disabled persons, and if necessary their families, about their rights and opportunities in the employment field; and

(b) overcoming prejudice, misinformation and attitudes unfavourable to the employment of disabled persons and their integration or reintegration into society.

17. Community leaders and groups, including disabled persons themselves and their organisations, should co-operate with health, social welfare, education, labour and other relevant government authorities in identifying the needs of disabled persons in the community and in ensuring that, wherever possible, disabled persons are included in activities and services available generally.

18. Vocational rehabilitation and employment services for disabled persons should be integrated into the mainstream of community development and where appropriate receive financial, material and technical support.

19. Official recognition should be given to voluntary organisations which have a particularly good record of providing vocational rehabilitation services and enabling disabled persons to be integrated or reintegrated into the worklife of the community.

IV. VOCATIONAL REHABILITATION IN RURAL AREAS

20. Particular efforts should be made to ensure that vocational rehabilitation services are provided for disabled persons in rural areas and in remote communities at the same level and on the same terms as those provided for urban areas. The development of such services should be an integral part of general rural development policies.

21. To this end, measures should be taken, where appropriate, to:

(a) designate existing rural vocational rehabilitation services or, if these do not exist, vocational rehabilitation services in urban areas as focal points to train rehabilitation staff for rural areas;

(b) establish mobile vocational rehabilitation units to serve disabled persons in rural areas and to act as centres for the dissemination of information on rural training and employment opportunities for disabled persons;

(c) train rural development and community development workers in vocational rehabilitation techniques;

(d) provide loans, grants or tools and materials to help disabled persons in rural communities to establish and manage co-operatives or to work on their own account in cottage industry or in agricultural, craft or other activities;
(e) incorporate assistance to disabled persons into existing or planned general rural development activities;
(f)   facilitate disabled persons' access to housing within reasonable reach of the workplace.

V. Training of Staff

22. In addition to professionally trained rehabilitation counsellors and specialists, all other persons who are involved in the vocational rehabilitation of disabled persons and the development of employment opportunities should be given training or orientation in rehabilitation issues.

23. Persons engaged in vocational guidance, vocational training and placement of workers generally should have an adequate knowledge of disabilities and their limiting effects, as well as a knowledge of the support services available to facilitate a disabled person's integration into active economic and social life. Opportunities should be provided for such persons to update their knowledge and extend their experience in these fields.

24. The training, qualifications and remuneration of staff engaged in the vocational rehabilitation and training of disabled persons should be comparable to those of persons engaged in general vocational training who have similar duties and responsibilities; career opportunities should be comparable for both groups of specialists and transfers of staff between vocational rehabilitation and general vocational training should be encouraged.

25. Staff of vocational rehabilitation, sheltered and production workshops should receive, as part of their general training and as appropriate, training in workshop management as well as in production and marketing techniques.

26. Wherever sufficient numbers of fully trained rehabilitation staff are not available, measures should be considered for recruiting and training vocational rehabilitation aides and auxiliaries. The use of such aides and auxiliaries should not be resorted to as a permanent substitute for fully trained staff. Wherever possible, provision should be made for further training of such personnel in order to integrate them fully into the trained staff.

27. Where appropriate, the establishment of regional and subregional vocational rehabilitation staff training centres should be encouraged.

28. Staff engaged in vocational guidance, vocational training, placement and employment support of disabled persons should have appropriate training and experience to recognise the motivational problems and difficulties that disabled persons may experience and, within their competence, deal with the resulting needs.

29. Where appropriate, measures should be taken to encourage disabled persons to undergo training as vocational rehabilitation personnel and to facilitate their entry into employment in the rehabilitation field.

30. Disabled persons and their organisations should be consulted in the development, provision and evaluation of training programmes for vocational rehabilitation staff.

VI. THE CONTRIBUTION OF EMPLOYERS' AND WORKERS' ORGANISATIONS TO THE DEVELOPMENT OF VOCATIONAL REHABILITATION SERVICES

31. Employers' and workers' organisations should adopt a policy for the promotion of training and suitable employment of disabled persons on an equal footing with other workers.

32. Employers' and workers' organisations, together with disabled persons and their organisations, should be able to contribute to the formulation of policies concerning the organisation and development of vocational rehabilitation services, as well as to carry out research and propose legislation in this field.

33. Wherever possible and appropriate, representatives of employers', workers' and disabled persons' organisations should be included in the membership of the boards and committees of vocational rehabilitation and training centres used by disabled persons, which make decisions on policy and technical matters, with a view to ensuring that the vocational rehabilitation programmes correspond to the requirements of the various economic sectors.

34. Wherever possible and appropriate, employers and workers' representatives in the undertaking should co-operate with appropriate specialists in considering the possibilities for vocational rehabilitation and job reallocation of disabled persons employed by that undertaking and for giving employment to other disabled persons.

35. Wherever possible and appropriate, undertakings should be encouraged to establish or maintain their own vocational rehabilitation services, including various types of sheltered employment, in close co-operation with community-based and other rehabilitation services.

36. Wherever possible and appropriate, employers' organisations should take steps to:

(a) advise their members on vocational rehabilitation services which could be made available to disabled workers;

(b) co-operate with bodies and institutions which promote the reintegration of disabled persons into active working life by providing, for instance, information on working conditions and job requirements which disabled persons have to meet;

(c) advise their members on adjustments which could be made for disabled workers to the essential duties or requirements of suitable jobs;

(d) advise their members to consider the impact that reorganising production methods might have, so that disabled persons are not inadvertently displaced.

37. Wherever poss ble and appropriate, workers' organisations should take steps to:

(a) promote the participation of disabled workers in discussions at the shop- floor level and in works councils or any other body representing the workers;

(b) propose guidelines for the vocational rehabilitation and protection of workers who become disabled through sickness or accident, whether work-related or not, and have such guidelines included in collective agreements, regulations, arbitration awards or other appropriate instruments;

(c) offer advice on shop-f oor arrangements affecting disabled workers, including job adaption, special work organisation, trial training and employment and the fixing of work norms;

(d) raise the problems of vocational rehabilitation and employment of disabled persons at trade union meetings and inform their members, through publications and seminars, of the problems of and possibilities for the vocational rehabilitation and employment of disabled persons.

VII. THE CONTRIBUTION OF DISABLED PERSONS AND THEIR
ORGANISATIONS TO THE DEVELOPMENT OF
VOCATIONAL REHABILITATION SERVICES

38. In addition to the participation of disabled persons, their representatives and organisations in rehabilitation activities referred to in Paragraphs 15, 17, 30, 32 and 33 of this Recommendation, measures to involve disabled persons and their organisations in the development of vocational rehabilitation services should include:

(a) encouragement of disabled persons and their organisations to participate in the development of community activities aimed at vocational rehabilitation of disabled persons so as to further their employment and their integration or reintegration into society;

(b) appropriate government support to promote the development of organisations of and for disabled persons and their involvement in vocational rehabilitation and employment services, including support for the provision of training programmes in self-advocacy for disabled persons;

(c) appropriate government support to these organisations to undertake public education programmes which project a positive image of the abilities of disabled persons.

VIII. VOCATIONAL REHABILITATION UNDER SOCIAL SECURITY SCHEMES

39. In applying the provisions of this Recommendation, Members should also be guided by the provisions of Article 35 of the Social Security (Minimum Standards) Convention, 1952, of Article 26 of the Employment Injury Benefits Convention, 1964, and of Article 13 of the Invalidity, Old-Age and Survivors' Benefits Convention, 1967, in so far as they are not bound by obligations arising out of ratification of these instruments.

40. Wherever possible and appropriate, social security schemes should provide, or contribute to the organisation, development and financing of training, placement and employment (including sheltered employment) programmes and vocational rehabilitation services for disabled persons, including rehabilitation counselling.

41. These schemes should also provide incentives to disabled persons to seek employment and measures to facilitate a gradual transition into the open labour market.

IX. CO-ORDINATION

42. Measures should be taken to ensure, as far as practicable, that policies and programmes concerning vocational rehabilitation are co-ordinated with policies and programmes of social and economic development (including scientific research and advanced technology) affecting labour administration, general employment policy and promotion, vocational training, social integration, social security, cooperatives, rural development, small-scale industry and crafts, safety and health at work, adaptation of methods and organisation of work to the needs of the individual and the improvement of working conditions.

Recommendation No. 99

RECOMMENDATION CONCERNING VOCATIONAL REHABILITATION OF THE DISABLED

The General Conference of the International Labour Organisation,

Having been convened at Geneva by the Governing Body of the International Labour Office, and having met in its Thirty-eighth Session on 1 June 1955, and

Having decided upon the adoption of certain proposals with regard to the vocational rehabilitation of the disabled, which is the fourth item on the agenda of the session, and

Having determined that these proposals shall take the form of a Recommendation,

adopts this twenty-second day of June of the year one thousand nine hundred and fifty-five, the following Recommendation, which may be cited as the Vocational Rehabilitation (Disabled) Recommendation, 1955:

Whereas there are many and varied problems concerning those who suffer disability, and

Whereas rehabilitation of such persons is essential in order that they be restored to the fullest possible physical, mental, social, vocational and economic usefulness of which they are capable, and

Whereas to meet the employment needs of the individual disabled person and to use manpower resources to the best advantage it is necessary to develop and restore the working ability of disabled persons by combining into one continuous and co-ordinated process medical, psychological, social, educational, vocational guidance, vocational training and placement services, including follow-up,

The Conference recommends as follows:

I. Definitions

1. For the purpose of this Recommendation –

(a) the term "vocational rehabilitation" means that part of the continuous and co-ordinated process of rehabilitation which involves the provision of those vocational services, e.g. vocational guidance, vocational training and selective placement, designed to enable a disabled person to secure and retain suitable employment; and

(b) the term "disabled person" means an individual whose prospects of securing and retaining suitable employment are substantially reduced as a result of physical or mental impairment.

II. Scope of Vocational Rehabilitation

2. Vocational rehabilitation services should be made available to all disabled persons, whatever the origin and nature of their disability and whatever their age, provided they can be prepared for, and have reasonable prospects of securing and retaining, suitable employment.

III. Principles and Methods of Vocational Guidance, Vocational Training and Placement of Disabled Persons

3. All necessary and practicable measures should be taken to establish or develop specialised vocational guidance services for disabled persons requiring aid in choosing or changing their occupations.

4. The process of vocational guidance should include, as far as practicable in the national circumstances and as appropriate in individual cases –

(a) interview with a vocational guidance officer;

(b) examination of record of work experience;

(c) examination of scholastic or other records relating to education or training received;

(d) medical examination for vocational guidance purposes;

(e) appropriate tests of capacity and aptitude, and, where desirable, other psychological tests;

(f) ascertainment of personal and family circumstances;

(g) ascertainment of aptitudes and the development of abilities by appropriate work experiences and trial, and by other similar means;

(h) technical trade tests, either verbal or otherwise, in all cases where such seem necessary;

(i) analysis of physical capacity in relation to occupational requirements and the possibility of mproving that capacity;

(j) provision of information concerning employment and training opportunities relating to the qualifications, physical capacities, aptitudes, preferences and experience of the person concerned and to the needs of the employment market.

5. The principles, measures and methods of vocational training generally applied in the training of non-disabled persons should apply to disabled persons in so far as medical and educational conditions permit.

6. (1) The training of disabled persons should, wherever possible, enable them to carry on an economic activity in which they can use their vocational qualifications or aptitudes in the light of employment prospects.

(2) For this purpose, such training should be –

(a) co-ordinated with selective placement, after medical advice, in occupations in which the performance of the work involved is affected by, or affects, the disability to the least possible degree;

(b) provided, wherever possible and appropriate, in the occupation in which the disabled person was previously employed or in a related occupation; and

(c) continued until the disabled person has acquired the skill necessary for working normally on an equal basis with non-disabled workers if he is capable of doing so.

7. Wherever possible, disabled persons should receive training with and under the same conditions as non-disabled persons.

8. (1) Special services should be set up or developed for training disabled persons who, particularly by reason of the nature or the severity of their disability, cannot be trained in company with non-disabled persons.

(2) Wherever possible and appropriate, these services should include, *inter alia*:

(a) schools and training centres, residential or otherwise;

(b) special short-term and long-term training courses for specific occupations;

(c) courses to increase the skills of disabled persons.

9. Measures should be taken to encourage employers to provide training for disabled persons; such measures should include, as appropriate, financial, technical, medical or vocational assistance.

10. (1) Measures should be taken to develop special arrangements for the placement of disabled persons.

(2) These arrangements should ensure effective placement by means of –

(a) registration of applicants for employment;

(b) recording their occupational qualifications, experience and desires;

(c) interviewing them for employment;

(d) evaluating, if necessary, their physical and vocational capacity;

(e) encouraging employers to notify job vacancies to the competent authority;

(f) contacting employers, when necessary, to demonstrate the employment capacities of disabled persons, and to secure employment for them;

(g) assisting them to obtain such vocational guidance, vocational training, medical and social services as may be necessary.

11. Follow-up measures should be taken –

(a) to ascertain whether placement in a job or recourse to vocational training or retraining services has proved to be satisfactory and to evaluate employment counselling policy and methods;

(b) to remove as far as possible obstacles which would prevent a disabled person from being satisfactorily settled in work.

IV. ADMINISTRATIVE ORGANISATION

12. Vocational rehabilitation services should be organised and developed as a continuous and co-ordinated programme by the competent authority or authorities and, in so far as practicable, use should be made of existing vocational guidance, vocational training and placement services.

13. The competent authority or authorities should ensure that an adequate and suitably qualified staff is available to deal with the vocational rehabilitation, including follow-up, of disabled persons.

14. The development of vocational rehabilitation services should at least keep pace with the development of the general services for vocational guidance, vocational training and placement.

15. Vocational rehabilitation services should be organised and developed so as to include opportunities for disabled persons to prepare for, secure and retain suitable employment on their own account in all fields of work.

16. Administrative responsibility for the general organisation and development of vocational rehabilitation services should be entrusted –

(a) to one authority, or

(b) jointly to the authorities responsible for the different activities in the programme with one of these authorities entrusted with primary responsibility for co-ordination.

17. (1) The competent authority or authorities should take all necessary and desirable measures to achieve co-operation and co-ordination between the public and private bodies engaged in vocational rehabilitation activities.

(2) Such measures should include as appropriate –

(a) determination of the responsibilities and obligations of public and private bodies;

(b) financial assistance to private bodies effectively participating in vocational rehabilitation activities; and

(c) technical advice to private bodies.

18. (1) Vocational rehabilitation services should be established and developed with the assistance of representative advisory committees, set up at the national level and, where appropriate, at regional and local levels.

(2) These committees should, as appropriate, include members drawn from among –

(a) the authorities and bodies directly concerned with vocational rehabilitation;

(b) employers' and workers' organisations;

(c) persons specially qualified to serve by reason of their knowledge of, and concern with, the vocational rehabilitation of the disabled; and

(d) organisations of disabled persons.

(3) These committees should be responsible for advising –

(a) at the national level, on the development of policy and programmes for vocational rehabilitation;

(b) at regional and local levels, on the application of measures taken nationally, their adaptation to regional and local conditions and the co-ordination of regional and local activities.

19. (1) Research should be fostered and encouraged, particularly by the competent authority, to evaluate and improve vocational rehabilitation services for the disabled.

(2) Such research should include continuous or special studies on the placement of the disabled.

(3)   Research should also include scientific work on the different techniques and methods which play a part in vocational rehabilitation.

V. Methods of Enabling Disabled Persons to Make Use of Vocational Rehabilitation Services

20. Measures should be taken to enable disabled persons to make full use of all available vocational rehabilitation services and to ensure that some authority is made responsible for assisting personally each disabled person to achieve maximum vocational rehabilitation.

21. Such measures should include –

(a) information and publicity on the availability of vocational rehabilitation services and on the prospects which they offer to the disabled;

(b) the provision of appropriate and adequate financial assistance to disabled persons.

22. (1) Such financial assistance should be provided at any stage in the vocational rehabilitation process and should be designed to facilitate the preparation for, and the effective retention of, suitable employment including work on own account.

(2) It should include the provision of free vocational rehabilitation services, maintenance allowances, any necessary transportation expenses incurred during any periods of vocational preparation for employment, and loans or grants of money or the supply of the necessary tools and equipment, and of prosthetic and any other necessary appliances.

23. Disabled persons should be enabled to make use of all vocational rehabilitation services without losing any social security benefits which are unrelated to their participation in these services.

24. Disabled persons living in areas having limited prospects of future employment or limited facilities for preparation for employment should be provided with opportunities for vocational preparation, including provision of board and lodging, and with opportunities for transfer, should they so desire, to areas with greater employment prospects.

25. Disabled persons (including those in receipt of disability pensions) should not as a result of their disability be discriminated against in respect of wages and other conditions of employment if their work is equal to that of non-disabled persons.

VI. CO-OPERATION BETWEEN THE BODIES RESPONSIBLE FOR MEDICAL TREATMENT AND THOSE RESPONSIBLE FOR VOCATIONAL REHABILITATION

26. (1) There should be the closest co-operation between, and the maximum co-ordination of, the activities of the bodies responsible for medical treatment and those responsible for the vocational rehabilitation of disabled persons.

(2) This co-operation and co-ordination of activities should exist —

(a) to ensure that medical treatment and, where necessary, the provision of appropriate prosthetic apparatus, are directed to facilitating and developing the subsequent employability of the disabled persons concerned;

(b) to promote the identification of disabled persons in need of, and suitable for, vocational rehabilitation;

(c) to enable vocational rehabilitation to be commenced at the earliest and most suitable stage;

(d) to provide medical advice, where necessary, at all stages of vocational rehabilitation;

(e) to provide assessment of working capacity.

27. Wherever possible, and subject to medical advice, vocational rehabilitation should start during medical treatment.

VII. METHODS OF WIDENING EMPLOYMENT OPPORTUNITIES FOR DISABLED PERSONS

28. Measures should be taken, in close co-operation with employers' and workers' organisations, to promote maximum opportunities for disabled persons to secure and retain suitable employment.

29. Such measures should be based on the following principles:

(a) disabled persons should be afforded an equal opportunity with the non-disabled to perform work for which they are qualified;

(b) disabled persons should have full opportunity to accept suitable work with employers of their own choice;

(c) emphasis should be placed on the abilities and work capacities of disabled persons and not on their disabilities.

30. Such measures should include –

(a) research designed to analyse and demonstrate the working capacity of disabled persons;

(b) widespread and sustained publicity of a factual kind with special reference to –

    (i) the work performance, output, accident rate, absenteeism and stability in employment of disabled persons in comparison with non-disabled persons employed in the same work;

    (ii) personnel selection methods based on specific requirements;

    (iii) methods of improving work conditions, including adjustment and modification of machinery and equipment, to facilitate the employment of disabled workers;

(c) the means whereby increased liability of individual employers in respect of workmen's compensation premiums may be eliminated;

(d) the encouraging of employers to transfer workers whose working capacity has undergone a change as a result of a physical impairment to suitable jobs within their undertakings.

31. Wherever appropriate in the national circumstances, and consistent with national policy, the employment of disabled persons should be promoted by means such as –

(a) the engagement by employers of a percentage of disabled persons under such arrangements as will avoid the displacement of non-disabled workers;

(b) reserving certain designated occupations for disabled persons;

(c) arranging that seriously disabled persons are given opportunities for employment or preference in certain occupations considered suitable for them;

(d) encouraging the creation and facilitating the operation of co-operatives or other similar enterprises managed by, or on behalf of, disabled persons.

VIII. Sheltered Employment

32. (1) Measures should be taken by the competent authority or authorities, in co-operation, as appropriate, with private organisations, to organise and develop arrangements for training and employment under sheltered conditions for those disabled persons who cannot be made fit for ordinary competitive employment.

(2) Such arrangements should include the establishment of sheltered workshops and special measures for those disabled persons who, for physical, psychological or geographical reasons, cannot travel regularly to and from work.

33. Sheltered workshops should provide, under effective medical and vocational supervision, not only useful and remunerative work but opportunities for vocational adjustment and advancement with, whenever possible, transfer to open employment.

34. Special programmes for the homebound should be so organised and developed as to provide, under effective medical and vocational supervision, useful and remunerative work in their own homes.

35. Where and to the extent to which statutory regulation of wages and conditions of employment applying to workers generally is in operation it should apply to disabled persons employed under sheltered conditions.

IX. SPECIAL PROVISIONS FOR DISABLED CHILDREN
AND YOUNG PERSONS

36. Vocational rehabilitation services for disabled children and young persons of school age should be organised and developed in close co-operation between the authorities responsible for education and the authority or authorities responsible for vocational rehabilitation.

37. Educational programmes should take into account the special problems of disabled children and young persons and their need of opportunities, equal to those of non-disabled children and young persons, to receive education and vocational preparation best suited to their age, abilities, aptitudes and interests.

38. The fundamental purposes of vocational rehabilitation services for disabled children and young persons should be to reduce as much as possible the occupational and psychological handicaps imposed by their disabilities and to offer them full opportunities of preparing for, and entering, the most suitable occupations. The utilisation of these opportunities should involve co-operation between medical, social and educational services and the parents or guardians of the disabled children and young persons.

39. (1) The education, vocational guidance, training and placement of disabled children and young persons should be developed within the general framework of such services to non-disabled children and young persons, and should be conducted, wherever possible and desirable, under the same conditions as, and in company with, non-disabled children and young persons.

(2) Special provision should be made for those disabled children and young persons whose disabilities prevent their participation in such services under the same conditions as, and in company with, non-disabled children and young persons.

(3) This provision should include, in particular, specialised training of teachers.

40. Measures should be taken to ensure that children and young persons found by medical examination to have disabilities or limitations or to be generally unfit for employment –

(a) receive, as early as possible, proper medical treatment for removing or alleviating their disabilities or limitations;

(b) are encouraged to attend school or are guided towards suitable occupations likely to be agreeable to them and within their capacity and are provided with opportunities of training for such occupations;

(c) have the advantage of financial aid, if necessary, during the period of medical treatment, education and vocational training.

X. APPLICATION OF THE PRINCIPLES OF VOCATIONAL REHABILITATION

41. (1) Vocational rehabilitation services should be adapted to the particular needs and circumstances of each country and should be developed progressively in the light of these needs and circumstances and in accordance with the principles laid down in this Recommendation.

(2) The main objectives of this progressive development should be –

(a) to demonstrate and develop the working qualities of disabled persons;

(b) to promote, in the fullest measure possible, suitable employment opportunities for them;

(c) to overcome, in respect of training or employment, discrimination against disabled persons on account of their disability.

42. The progressive development of vocational rehabilitation services should be promoted with the help, where desired, of the International Labour Office –

(a) by the provision, wherever possible, of technical advisory assistance;

(b) by organising a comprehensive international exchange of experience acquired in different countries; and

(c) by other forms of international co-operation directed towards the organisation and development of services adapted to the needs and conditions of individual countries and including the training of the staff required.

Printed in

CINTERFOR
Montevideo - Uruguay

D.L.: 330.692/2003

www.ingramcontent.com/pod-product-compliance
Lightning Source LLC
Chambersburg PA
CBHW031218270326
41931CB00006B/604